Live Life
with Love.

The ideas expressed in the book are those of the author. Any resemblance to actual persona, living or dead, is purely coincidental, where not clearly stated.

Book Cover and Interior Design by Stanley Dumanig

Front page photo by Eli Smith

Published in Canada by Victoria Vienna Publishing
150 Bamburgh Circle, Toronto, M1W 3V7
ON

ISBN: 978-0-9812494-1-4

VICTORIA VIENNA
PUBLISHING
**www.VictoriaViennaPublishing.com**

**Printed in Canada**

# Soothe My Soul

# A Note of Thanks

The gratitude I feel towards the wonderful people who, over the years, have encouraged me to publish this book of poetry, is beyond words. Thank you all for your support, feedback and especially a big thanks to my publisher, Giselle of Victoria-Vienna Publishing, for reaching out to me and showing me that this was possible.

Above all I thank God for bringing me through a difficult time in my life and for birthing these words out of such sorrow.

I hope and pray as you read these words, recorded on paper, you will be able to feel and relate to the pain within the struggles of life and draw some strength from its joys and triumphs.

Patrick O. Morris

# Publisher's Note

The word Adhan, in Arabic means "call to prayer". In Islam, the Muezzin, one who performs the call to prayer, recites the Adhan over a loud speaker and all around the world, countless people, in voluntary obedience, descend upon their local mosque to pray. Adhan comes from the root word 'adhina' meaning "to listen, to hear, or to be informed about."

The words of Patrick Morris are like a call to prayer for me, not in a religious sense; however, like a call to prayer, his words call my emotions forth, and in almost hypnotic obedience, they go to a special place to receive solace. In my opinion, this is not a book to be read, but to be experienced. I got the most out of it when I breathed it in, held it, and let its vapors permeate my cells.

I would suggest you do the same, and perhaps allow yourself to fully experience whatever emotions arise. Inhale deeply, then, slowly exhale his words. Let them marinate your soul. Perhaps you'll escape into a reality you've been denying. Maybe you'll remember things you've forgotten to appreciate like your children, friends, God, and the world around you. You may even gain insight into things you've never considered before.

Go ahead. Get intimate and scholastic with it. Mark it up. Get out your highlighter and your pen. Make notes. Ear mark pages, or add your own exclamation marks. Let your tear drops stain the page.

Love it. Use it. Let it go. Get grossed in the mind of Patrick Morris.

Giselle M. Medford

# Table of Contents

**mis·cel·la·ne·ous**

**Patrick Morris**
January 23

By Love

By love I am destroyed
By love I am saved
By love I am recreated
The fortitude I require
To look love in the face and be transformed
Into something greater than I was before
Is the compelling force
I must embrace in order to be more than I am
I dare to love in the face of anger
Frustration and shame
His love not always apparent
At times like the sun hidden behind the clouds
It's visibility lacking on a rainy day
But Loves reality is forever unfailing....

Like · Comment · Share 10 1

10 people like this.

**Giselle Medford** Book! Book! We gotta get on this this year 🙂 Was busy finishing my Masters Degree but this year is OURS!! g.
January 23 at 9:30am · Like · 1

Yep, it was; and we finally did it.
We hope you enjoy.

Always,

# mis·cel·la·ne·ous

pronounced: /ˌmisəˈlānēəs/

*adjective*

1. (of items or people gathered or considered together) of various types or from different sources.

2. (of a collection or group) composed of members or elements of different kinds.

## My Words

The explicit expressions of my words
Provide verbal intercourse to your soul
The intimacy I create
Through the blueprint of my meditations
Are filled with irresistible
Wondrous expressions of affection
Like lightning breaking through the stormy skies
My thunder destroys the silence
My words plunge to the depths of your soul
Even into your hidden places
Openness, truth, sincerity and honesty
Are the tools of my trade
My words can't be denied

**The Adventure of Love**

The adventure of love is never what we think
It comes to us in ways we do not expect
The universe unfolds
And
The journey is filled with many curves
Twists and surprises
The journey of love is greater
Than the destination
It is the exploration of a lifetime
I seek to enjoy everyday of my journey
With openness
Humility
The willingness to learn
Embracing
All the lessons my journey in love
Has to offer
One day at a time

## Springtime

The Springtime sun liquefies the winter frost
With anticipation
Of blossoms to come
We
Await the thaw
Shattering the earth
We free ourselves
From the bondage of ice and snow
First the flower
Then the fruits of our labor
Are savored
Embracing you
Is the springtime sun on my face
Awakening my passion?
My desire for you
Is
Like a springtime flower now in full bloom

**The Wolf**

There are wolves that surround us
They stalk us
Seeking to devour us
The inexplicable truth is
That sheep must face these wolves daily
The key is to accept that the wolf is a wolf
Face the wolf without fear
Understand their nature
Face the wolf with love
Be powerful enough
Not to allow the wolf to change who you are
Change you into something you are not
Often, we seek to protect ourselves from the wolf
By being like the wolf
Not wanting to be destroyed
We build walls to isolate ourselves
The fear of getting hurt
Outweighs our natural nature to be sheep
Be the wise sheep
Continue to stand without fear
Embrace love and give love
With no remorse

**Friendship**

The bonds of friendship
Run deep
Knows no boundaries
Nor shame
Pure and undiluted
The only tie that binds
Together those whose choice
Is to embrace fellowship
This choice
Not taken lightly
Requires unfailing
Cultivation

**Unique**

The unusual
Unconventional
Unexpected
Eccentric
Different
Not the norm
This is the reality of the imprint left within my thoughts
Who knew?
Who would expect such illumination
Such Beauty
That is clearly
Beyond
The deepness of your skin
Allowing another to see the simplicity
Within the humility of your thoughts?
The fearless ability
You have to be yourself
Without façade
Refreshing
Inspiring

**Intimacy and Communion**

To know me
Is to know intimacy and communion
The connection my soul creates with you is unique
Passionate
Pure
Undiluted
Powerful
And
Intoxicating
Some fear it and run
Some seek to embrace it
Yet I restrain them
For they fall short
Like junkies
They run the risk of becoming an addict
Ever seeking the next hit
Some seek to create intimacy with sex
They are disillusioned
By this vision of splendor
Sex is not intimacy
Some seek to feed from my fruit
They believe this is communion
They are surprised
This is not intimacy or communion
Intimacy is
To let me in
Behind your mask
Allowing me access to the child within your soul
Sharing your fears, pains and desires
And becoming vulnerable
Allowing me to handle your soul with care
Communion is a mutual giving and receiving
The feeding of souls

I feed you
You feed me
We become something greater than we could be alone
Just as parents
Both contribute to the process
Sperm
Egg
Life is created
And
The creation is greater than the individual
So does communion get created through intimacy
Creating something greater than you or me

## I am Arrested

I am arrested
By the beauty that is the twinkle
Within your eyes
As you smile at me
Your teeth glisten
Like perfect cut diamonds
I am incarcerated
By your faith in me
Unwavering
Trusting
Limitless
Your love is the fuel
Allowing my soul to thrive
I freely surrender myself
To you
As you grant me access
To knowing the woman
Within

## Exposed

Once Pandora's Box is opened
And the Genie
In the bottle is revealed
What does one do?
Many of us
Struggle to close the door of the closet
While we try to keep
The exposed bones from falling out
What if
Instead of hiding things in the closet
We opened the doors
Tossed away the bones
Swept the floors
And allowed
The sunshine in?
Until we our clean house
We will never be free from our restraints

**Seeds We Sow**

The days of men and women
On this planet earth are numbered
Remember at some point
We all must harvest
The rewards
Blessings
Shame
Or
Famine
From the seeds we sow
Within our lives
And in the lives of others

## Redwood

Allowing yourself to love
Without fear
Shame
Never withholding
Yet forever giving freely
Is only the seed
You must still till the land
Then plant the seed
Water the ground
Protect the sprout
From vermin and the elements
So too will your
Faith
Love
And confidence grow
Like a mighty Redwood
Standing the test of time
Weathering the storms of life
Conquering all of the challenges life has to offer

## Call to Action

We must start at the beginning with the key
The economic masters of old
Recognized that consumerism was the key to enslave a nation
We must respond in-kind
Recognizing the key to freeing a nation
For hundreds of years we moved from disillusion to despondency
Ultimately to depression
Unknowingly
Unwillingly
Passing on the seeds of mental slavery throughout the generations
However
The writing is now on the wall
We must not only read the writing but must do the work to stop the cycle
Providing the tools necessary to break the psychological chains
This priority no one else can deliver
These chains have created a society of emotionally challenged individuals
Caught up in the illusion that being obsessed with monetary gains
Is that what it means to be human?
Regardless of how this illusion was acquired
These challenges we face
Do not afford us the ability to respect one another
Care for our children or ourselves
Or the spiritual necessities of life
I put a call out to the Community
To the so called Leaders, Pastors, Ministers, Teachers,
Mothers, Fathers, Brothers, Sisters, Uncles, Aunts
I call on everyone in earshot to step up
Stand strong
Show the way
Be the light
Hold your head high
And say I am more
I am a man
I am a woman
I am Godlike

I deserve and will do better than I see
I will give
Not back
But forward
If not you
Then who?
If not now
Then when?
Pick up your daily cross
and
You may be the last expression of God
another gets to see

## A Seasoned Life

A seasoned life
Love without measure
Nor regret
Commitment in companionship
Emotionally and intellectually evolved
Nurturer of many souls
A legacy fulfilled
Freely delivered
To offspring
Shared with friends and the world
Respected by all
Teacher
Lover
Friend
Fearless
Confident
Selfless
The aged who have a seasoned life
Share wisdom with those who
Would have an ear to listen

## Our Faith

Our faith defines us
The beliefs we hold dear
Are expressions
Of our ability to share ourselves
With each other
With those close to us and far removed
Regardless of our spiritual commitment
One truth binds us all together
The truth that
We must love one another
Do good to each other
Provide to those without
After all, we are all keepers of each other
On this planet Earth

## Enjoy Laughter

A life without laughter
Is like the depths of the ocean
Cold
Filled with pressure
Volcanic eruptions
And
Darkness
Release the pressure
Find your joy
And
Enjoy laughter

## Let Truth

Let truth flow from your lips
Like sunshine
In darkness
Let truth from your lips
Illuminate the paths of untruths
Let it shine
To those around you
And free
Their souls from darkness
Let the truth pursue
Fear
Distrust
Unbelief
And
Slay it

**We Commune**

The bond of mental communication
Cultivated and stimulated
By intimacy
Is created daily
As our souls commune
We are renewed
This relationship is like the vastness of the ocean
Limitless as the universe
This union is greater
Than the individual components
Of you or me
We sit in reverence to its power
Without fear

**Create a New Beginning**

The end is never the end
But a new beginning
For those who embrace change
Life is never about right or wrong
It is and will always be about choices
If what you chose did not work the way you wanted
Start something new
Create a new beginning
By making a new choice
The new beginning is often bitter sweet
The challenge is
Not allowing
The bitter to outweigh the sweet
The sweet is never hard to find
If you are ready to taste it
And do not fear it

## Rewards of Change

The big-bang set in motion
The unimaginable relentless evolution
We call change
To fight this monumental force that encompasses our lives
Is to embrace madness
As a boy must become a man and a girl a woman
Change is the natural state of our existence
We must all embrace it
Let go of yesterday
Embrace the now
Prepare for tomorrow
And
Enjoy the rewards of change

## Your Path

There is a plan for our life
We all must fulfill
How we accomplish this plan
Is the path we must choose
Going left, right
Doing something or nothing
Embracing or fighting
The journey
Is your choice
All things will work together for good
For those who choose
To find the goodness within the path
To the destination

**Vending Machine of Life**

As you stand before the vending machine of life
With choices
What will you do
To ensure you have the correct change that is required?
Remember
The anxiety you may feel
Is an illustration
Of your ability to make change
You change your
Car
Home
Cell phone
Gadgets
Jobs
Even Partners
But you still have fear
How long will you allow others
To benefit from your inability to make change?
Why fear the change that really matters?
You struggle to make the changes
Within your life that will benefit you
Putting off what needs to be completed
Holding back
When you should be letting go…
Embrace the change
Allowing you to find
Freedom

**Misunderstandings and Expectations**

The misunderstandings of your expectations
Are a direct representation
Of your shortcomings
Your inability to take another for their reality
When you assume
They will live up to your expectations
This inevitable disaster was created by you
And you cannot avoid
I strive
Each day to live up to my own expectations
Allowing others
To show me their reality
by bringing into existence
What is within their heart
Without the misunderstandings of my expectations

## Reflection of Self

My reflection of self
Awakens my desire to be more than I am
As sun rays bring
Warmth to the first buds of springtime
The anticipation of blossoms
Sweet nectar
With the potential of ripe fruit
To nourish the body
So does my soul shatter the bondage
Of
Fear, uncertainty and hesitation
I embrace my gifts
Freely on display
For the world to see
As I am renewed

## Is There a Worm in Your Apple?

Your value of self
Is beyond the depth of the beauty of your skin
A gleaming red apple
Is seductive
However
It is of no value when infested with parasites
Anyone with skin-deep beauty can attract a mate
The question is how long will they stay
When they see the parasites hidden within
It requires strength of character
Confidence in one's self
The ability to face yourself
Naked within the mirror
Critiquing your imperfection
Facing your demons
Without fear
Removing the parasites
Of bondage
Disposing of old luggage
Freeing the soul
And
Committing, spiritually

**Demonstrating Your Character**

The actions you share with your fellow citizens of this planet earth
Are an accurate demonstration of your character
Your fellow citizens
Judge you
Based on the strength of your character
And your ability to reveal
Your strength
When faced with the actions
Of others
You may not agree with these actions
But it is your responsibility
To exhibit your strength of character
When darkness thrives
How else will your light be discovered

**Quality of Life**

The length of time of your life on this planet
Is predetermined
And
Is measured by the quality
You bring into existence
Eating to live
Or
Living to eat
Is a choice
Seeing the physician
Taking your medication
Allowing stress to rule your life
Choices we all face
Working to live
Or
Living to work
These things predetermine the length of time of ones life
On this planet earth
What steps will you take to determine
The quality of your life?

## Mirror

The misunderstandings of self-focus
Self-gratification
And
False expectations
Are based on your inability
To see
Your own weaknesses
When you see
The flaws of others
See them
With the understanding
That you are looking
At your reflection

**We. Are. They**

They say the truth is out there
But who are they?
And where is there?
We walk through life missing
The fact that "they"
Are you and me
And "there"
Is here
Right now
It is easy to become detached from the truth
When we see the world as "us" and "them"
As we continue to fear each other
We lose the connection that is our humanity
The truth is
Right here
Right now
You and me
We are the same
No more
No less

## The Earth is Crying

The Earth is angry
At the virus called humanity
Out of control
We are a cancer
Devouring everything in our path
How can we blame the Earth's immune system?
Like a surgeon's blade
Its scalpel removes the cancer
With
Earth quakes
Cyclones
Hurricanes
Ice and snow
We lament in the face of tragedy
Yet do nothing
To relieve the suffering of the Earth
She cries
But no one is listening
We forget we are but parasites
Requiring the Earth's body
For survival
This symbiotic relationship
Requires balance

**I See You**

I see you
Your dedication
Determination
Your unyielding focus
To be better is a gift
I see your struggle
I see your pain
The parent you are standing strong
Sacrifices embraced
The trustworthy friend, selfless and giving
The professional you manifest daily
Standing in the midst of challenges
The student of life
Continuously seeking knowledge, wisdom and understanding
Your focus on the prize
Never wavers
Your fathomless convictions
The essential fortitude necessary to ascend all obstacles
The lessons you teach
Continue to stand strong
For
These gifts are not unnoticed
I see you my friend
I see you

# chil·dren

pronounced: 'CHildrən

*noun*

1. Plural of child
2. a young human being below the age of puberty or below the legal age of majority.
    - a son or daughter of any age.

**Teach Your Children**

How do you know freedom?
When all you have lived is
Destruction
Devastation
War
And
Restraint
How does a man know
How to be a man to a woman
Without a man to teach him?
How does a woman know
How to be a woman
To a man
Without a woman to teach her?
We sell ourselves short
By being examples
To our children
Of people we do not want them to be
The children need to see
What is right
We need to stand in the midst of our adversity
And teach them
How else will they learn?
They are God's gift to you
On loan for a time
Take care of the gift

**My Children**

The pride I realize
When I look into the eyes of my children
Is like none other
I see the reflections
I have helped them to appreciate about themselves
Others
And
The world around them
The understanding
Of what is required for life on this planet we call Earth
This is my reward
I look forward to them continuing
To harvest all the benefits
God has in store for them
And
I can deliver to them
Daily

## Be Like the Children

The inner strength that is within us all
Many of us have forgetten
Sadly as we age we learn
Fear
Mistrust
Wickedness
Imagine for a moment
If we learned how to maintain
Our ability to give unconditional love
With no attachments
As children do
Imagine what this world would be like…
Forgiveness
And
No grudges
We would trust
I strive to live each day
To remember my childish ways
And
Love with childlike abandon

## Fatherhood

As you enter this chapter called fatherhood remember
This new life you have been blessed with
Is not yours to control or manipulate
But the soul you have been entrusted with
Is on loan to you
God above has provided you the perfect gift
The gift to nurture a life
You are the facilitator of this next generation
Your legacy will be left on this planet
Based on how well you share your soul with your gift
Remember that the man you are
Is more than enough for this task at hand
God decided to give you this task
Remember
In your darkest hour
No matter how hard the struggle
Continue to let your light shine
So your gift will see
The lighthouse you are through storms of life
Let your light shine
As you embrace and enjoy
The journey that is
Fatherhood

## Youth

The beauty in the expression of youth
Realized
Nurtured
Into maturity
Unbridled
Once released into the universe
Is limitless
It captivates the spirit within
Embrace your self-expression
Within the love that is God
With the curiosity of a child
Let relentless passion and his Holy Spirit
Lead you to answers
But
Never forget to
Forgive with childlike innocence
Be fearless
For the world is your play ground

**Fathers and Mothers**

The life of some fathers and mothers
Is filled with sweet sorrow
And
Overflowing with an abundance of joy
Some never understand the
Joy that binds parent to child
Those fathers and mothers
Who are fathers and mothers
For the wrong reasons
Will never know
The power in shaping and guiding this mind
The fathers and mothers who understand
Stand strong
You may not see the fruits of your toil
But others will be filled
And blessed

**Childlike**

To understand the meaning of life
Is to see the world through the eyes of a child
Full of wonder
Hope
Faith
Love
And the innocence in forgiveness
As we age
We forget our childlike ways
We become disconnected
From our fellow citizens of planet earth
We learn
Mistrust
Hate
Anger
Self-control
Fear
Good and evil
We can learn a lot
As we take time
To look into the eyes of a child
Remembering how to love with childlike innocence
Embracing the purity
Letting go
And
Forgiving

## L·amour

*noun*
1. An intense feeling of deep affection.
2. a person or thing that one loves.

*verb*
feel a deep romantic or sexual attachment to (someone).

 58 | Soothe My Soul

## Reflections of You

Reflections of you water my heart
The twinkle I see in your eyes
As you look into my soul
Fuels my spark into an inferno
I embrace you
Wanting to know the little girl inside your soul
Behind the mask
Beyond the wall
Until there is no wall
Creating oneness
Where spirits share
Until we exist as individuals no more
More than an addiction to a drug
But only the reality
That we do not wish to live
Without watering each other's souls
Until that day comes
I sit in earnest anticipation
As we add
Logs to our fire

## I Guide

Holding your hand
I guide you to the secret places within my soul
You enter my chambers of love
With appreciation and admiration
Allowing you to sit at the banquet of my love
Until your cup overflows
You are
Immersed within a state of happiness
Knowing the pleasures of
Companionship and intellectual stimulation
We are satisfied as one

## Your Voice

With hands lifted high and my eyes to the sky
I sit in the drought of your silence
Awaiting a word
I wait for your thoughts to become
The sound of your precious voice
Oh how I love the sound of your voice
Your voice is the rain that fills the parched earth of my soul with moisture
Your voice awakens wondrous new life within me
Your voice flows into many rivers becoming a mighty force
Filling me with joy
Your voice has power to create something out of nothing
This power to breathe new life where life once lived
To see beyond my parched Earth
Envisioning the lush valley that is my soul
How did you know my valley needed the rain
That is your sweet voice?

**We Awake**

We awake with desire
Not wanting to leave each other
Without a word our thoughts are known
We communicate on a level
Others seek
But never find
I am a star
You are the very essence of the universe
You encompass me
I light your path
You comfort my nights
With no fear
Hesitation
Nor wavering
Your willingness to be one with me
Can only be compared
To my quenchless thirst
To be one with you

## I Am Humbled

Your words fill me with hope
The universe set our path in motion
Before the existence of time
The universe prepared you for me and me for you
Shaping and molding our experiences
Preparing us for this meeting
How can a man and a woman fight destiny?
To see your smile
See beyond your eyes
I am humbled by your touch
Wanting to spend each moment with you
Time is canceled when I am in your presence
Sharing your space
To breathe your air
To know my breath is your breath
Your life is my life
How can this humble man be so blessed
To encounter a woman such as you?
I shall spend a lifetime showing you your imprint on my soul
Your essence has captivated me
The universe knew what it was doing
When it made you and me

## I Have Questions

Good morning love
I awake with thoughts of you
I can't help but wonder
Why have you distanced yourself from me?
Have I offended you in some way?
Did I do something to make you uncomfortable?
Was our last encounter not favorable?
I look forward to getting your texts each day
It brightens my path
I love the sound of your voice
It is music to me
I miss you
Do you miss me?
Am I alone in the connection we shared?
Tell me
You awoke something in me
I hope to see no end
Wanting to know who you are deep inside
Who is the little girl within?
I wonder

## This Inexplicable Thing

The aroma that is your scent
On my pillow
Reminding me of the moments we share
The embrace
Your tenderness and strength
The confidence
You offer this man
Like the Sirens of Greece
Singing their alluring songs
You are captivating
Drawing me in
Like sweet nectar from heaven
The gods of Olympus created
This inexplicable thing we share called love
To hold you
Caress you
Taste you
To indulge myself within you
Savoring your scent is as close to Heaven
A man can come without leaving earth
This love is beyond physical gratification
Flawless
Two souls
One heartbeat without fear

## Sun/Moon

Trapped in the eternal struggle
The Sun yearns to look upon the face of his Moon
The Moon waits with desire
The enviable decay of her night
Allowing the dawning of her morning Sun
As the Sun awakes from his slumber
He knows he must bow down
Allowing his Moon to bring forth
The fullness of her night
Their eyes meet for moments
She basks in his light
He takes rest in the arms of her night
Enjoying every moment

**Your Beauty**

Your beauty is much more than skin deep
It is a fresh water spring breaking through the earth
Bringing forth life
Washing away the impurities of past burdens from my soul
Renewing my faith in love
In humanity
Your beauty is beyond me
Within me as I am in you
Your beauty is in your sacrifice
It is your ability to see beyond my flaws
The broken mess of the man I was
Yet you love me
You refresh me
I drink from the spring that is your beauty
You give me love
And
Strength to carry on

**Keys**

If you offered me the keys to your soul
Willingly without fear
I would hide it within
The deepest places of my soul
I would rejoice
I would shout from on high
For all to see my admiration of you
I rejoice
Exalting you above the stars
The world would see the light that has captivated me
My love for you
Cannot be measured
It has no beginning
No end
This love
Is a gift from the gods

## Waiting

I await the day our eyes will meet
Again for the first time
Remembering you
Dominates my thoughts
Deep beyond the fortified wall
That is my comfort
You exposed my soul
No restraint
Willingly I permit
You access to the boy within
Thrilling
Dangerous
Is my craving for you
No fan or current of air
Is required
To intensify the flames of passion
Nor the affection between us
I await the day our eyes will meet again for the first time
With patience

## I Gaze

The Bird of Paradise in full bloom
Is your elegance
I am drawn to you
Like a hummingbird
To nectar
The exquisiteness of your movements
Are Shakespearian in nature
Fathomless humility
Loveliness is your soul
Your virtue revealed to me
As I gaze through the windows that are your eyes

**Beauty Flows**

To gaze on your beauty
Is to gaze upon Heaven itself
The beauty that is you, is unlike another
It flows from within your soul
This phenomenon is unique to you
I am content to be in your presence
What is this beauty that flows from you?
How does one place value on something so priceless?
Like a moth to the flame
So do those around you flock to your beauty
This precious gift
The universe has given you, is not to be taken lightly
It can not be ignored
It must be displayed on the mountain top
For the world to see and appreciate
This beauty enlightens paths
Provides comfort to weary and lost souls
To gaze upon your beauty
Is to gaze upon Heaven itself
None is more thankful than I
To have this gift
The universe has brought to me
None is more blessed

**Creation of Our Love**

Before the earth was fashioned out of nothingness
I loved you
Before the design within the womb
Was shaped into the life that became you
I loved you
Before I knew you
I loved you
The day our eyes met was predetermined
For God created
You for me and I for you
The inevitable meeting of our souls
Was set in motion
The moment the universe emerged from its slumber
The formality of our meeting
Insignificant
God created this love
Between us before the existence of us
Each, not-so-random act,
Shaped our lives
They created the man I am
The woman you are
God made you for me and I for you

**Morning**

Your hair partially covers your face
As the morning sun breaks through the window
The sunlight pales in contrast to your beauty
I examine
The way your lips come together
They form a perfect smile
Not yet awake
I take inventory of you
Your closed eyes
Fill me with wonder
Dreams of our succulent fruit
Dipped in dark chocolate
Rich cream
Sweetened and dripping
With honey

## Coupled

My independence gives way
To interdependence
As our souls cross the threshold of spiritual union
The symbiotic relationship we create
Is coupled within
The deepest depths of our souls
Your love for me is without borders
Endless
My love for you
Allows me to be fearless
Opening my soul
You enter
We share our secret places
Without constraint
We submerge ourselves
Within the freedom that is our love

**I Love You**

Your touch overloads
The electrochemical signaling within my nervous system
Highlighting my inability to express in words
The emotions I feel when you lay next to me
Watching you sleep
I fight my selfish desires
To wake you yet again
From your slumber
Listening to the sounds of your breathing
Peacefully
I recall the passion
The fire of no less than an hour ago
I whisper three words in your ear
You awake with a smile

**Senses**

I taste the unimaginable flavors
Of your lips
Inhaling your intoxicating fragrance
You overpower my intellect
I am witness
To
The waters of your rivers
Freshly awoken
Flowing from your crimson peaks
You are captive
To the pleasures of my explorations
I discover every detail
That is your composition
Your hidden jewels
Exposed to the elements of my nature
Raw
Powerful
And all encompassing

## Don't Wonder

I remember how your nose wrinkled
When you laughed at my attempts at humor
I remember the surprise
I saw in your eyes
As you evaluated the maturity of my character
Was this an act?
Was he real?
I see your wonderings
What is this ability he has
To facilitate the surrendering of himself
Effortlessly
Expressing the essence of his being
Freely
Liberating himself
From judgment
Casting off the restraints of expectations
Don't wonder
This ability I have is because
You naturally see into my soul
Allowing me to be

## Pleasure and Pain

Standing in the midst of your love
I undergo pleasure and pain
You pull me close
And push me away
At the same time
With confusion
I embrace you
Holding you close
Letting you know
All is well within our world
The tension of your fear is vast
Your love for me is enduring
Yet the fear of opening the door to your soul is grand
I open my heart
You must see the purity of my honesty
You find comfort in the strength of my arms
The warm place I create for you within my soul
Is enough to take away your fear
You open your soul
You give yourself freely

## Standing Equal

Loving you
Highlights my insufficiency
The vastness and luminance of the universe
Is dimmed by the beauty that is you
This beauty overshadows me
Is overwhelming and all encompassing
You confirm my inadequateness
Is a fabrication of my imagination
I bow down in reverence to your beauty
You stop me
You elevate me to stand with you
You educate me
That I am more than enough to satisfy you
Using your power over me
You show your admiration for my manliness
You show me myself as you see me
Through your eyes
In turn
I see my power over you
We stand equal

**Bodies Intertwine**

What would the experience be
When our eyes meet
Enjoying the lusciousness of our fruit
The expression of oneness
Our senses heightened
Overloaded with the sweet flavor of our lips
I draw you close
You encompass me
All of me
My unyielding desire for you
Your selfless pursuit to water my soul
Explodes from within you and is expressed outwards
My quenchless starvation for you is never filled
We taste the fruit from our trees
Our fruit is mature and ready to be consumed
The embers that burn within our souls
Now ablaze with fuel from our trees
The fire is great
We burn with desire
The anticipation of my entry
You hold me close
Your body yearns from within
Not yet
I whisper in your ear
I want to hear your heart sing a love song
Sing a song it never sang before
You sing with a great voice
The sounds of our love
It's time for us to...

**Smitten**

In bed alone
Neither asleep nor awake
With thoughts of you
Who are you that captivated me?
Looking into your eyes
Was like seeing myself for the first time
Anticipation
Weakness
Longing and desire
Something unexplainable
As you looked at me
Your lips came together
To form a perfect beam of light
That is your smile
Seeing your smile
Penetrating
Touching deep within my soul
Being next to you is bitter sweet agony
One touch
The ignition is lit
The very sight of you brought back memories
From a time lost long ago
Yet freshly awakened
Your embrace facilitated emotions beyond measure
I am smitten by your love

## My Woman

Your capacity for compassion
Love
Understanding
Is as great as the depths of the ocean
Your will to give yourself freely
Openly
Is childlike
Restriction-less
Overwhelming
All encompassing
Your desire to satisfy me is unbridled
Your openness to grow
Is as the sun breaking through the clouds
Of a winter storm
Your selflessness to give
To your children
The world
Is immeasurable
The only comparison to your vastness
Is my fortitude
My willingness to serve you
My desire to give you the stars
My undying quenchless thirst to give you my soul
I enlighten your spirit
Like the morning sun
Chases away the darkness of night
As you refresh me
With dewdrops from your lips

## 7 Days Until Our Eyes Meet Again for the First Time
## Day1

As I wake this glorious morning I realize
The sadness I feel is both bitter and sweet
I know you are near to me but so very far away
I am accustomed to hearing your voice each morning
The sound of your voice is lightning at midnight
Lighting my path and giving me hope
Hope in humanity
Hope in women
Hope to feel again
Each day with you makes me a believer
The light you bring to my life
Astounds me day by day
Just days until I see you again
Just days until I hear the sweet sound of your voice
I hope this day brings you much joy
Until our eyes meet again for the first time

## 7 Days Until Our Eyes Meet Again for the First Time
## Day2

I went to bed last night wondering if you missed me
Was I far from your thoughts?
Did you hold me in your heart?
Do you wonder if I miss you?
Let there be no doubt
No question
No trepidation
Just the simple truth that
The Superman I am
Misses the Wonder Woman
You are
Just a little bit of time
Until our eyes meet again for the first time

## 7 Days Until Our Eyes Meet Again for the First Time
## Day3

I awake this morning
With the imprint of your smile in my mind
Remembering how you gaze at me
Tempted yet reserved
When you look into my eyes
Do you see yourself as I see you?
Can you see the joy your smile brings to me?
A simple smile
Your smile ignites the anticipation
Of many possibilities
Just a little bit of time
Until our eyes meet again for the first time

**7 Days Until Our Eyes Meet Again for the First Time**
**Day 4**

No MSN
@ Work is off line
No txt msg
Nobody home
No Blackberry
No Cell Phone
No Emails
Man… if I send a smoke signal will you get it?
I must await your return
Just a little bit of time
Until our eyes meet again for the first time

## 7 Days Until Our Eyes Meet Again for the First Time
## Day 5

When you meet someone
Who has the potential to radically change your world
Shift you off balance
See your soul and make you change direction
What does one do?
Should we
Fear it
Run from it
Embrace it
How does a man and woman
Attempt to manage an attraction that is
Primeval
Natural
Raw
And oh so powerful
How does one say no or yes
With so many variables
Just a little bit of time
Until our eyes meet again for the first time

**7 Days Until Our Eyes Meet Again for the First Time**
**Day 6**

What are these feelings
You awake within me?
To see lips
I have never truly kissed
And crave for them
Yearning to hold someone
I have never truly held
To miss a smell
I have never truly inhaled
What are these feelings
You have awakened within me?
Are you longing for me?
Have I awakened them in you?
Will we explore them?
Just a little bit of time
Until we meet again for the first time

## 7 Days Until Our Eyes Meet Again for the First Time
## Day 7

You ignited
Memories of childhood
Memories of a first crush
Memories of a first kiss
Memories of the innocence of forgotten youth
Who are you that has enchanted me
With the very sight of you?
Your touch fills me with excitement
Just a few short moments
Until we meet again for the first time

**Ripe Fruit**

Eyes meet
Bodies entangled
The delectable
Expression of togetherness
Senses overloaded
With flavor of succulence
Pulling you in
You clinch me
My never ending pursuit of your happiness
Is expressed moment by moment
Time apart has ripened our crop
I acquire the fruit
You seize mine
Our fruit well-seasoned
Is being enjoyed

## Glory of Love

To gaze into the eyes of love
In all its glory
And not be transformed
Into something greater than you were before
Is the impossibility
We understand as we evolve
To embrace love within your soul
Is walking with no fear or hesitation
It is to give of yourself freely
Confidently
Completely
Without conditions
The love you give
Will not be based on the conditions of another
Give freely
Because you love...

## Music of Love

You are the music of my soul
Like melody
Blowing across the wind
The strings of an acoustic guitar
Cannot compare
To the sounds of our sweet love
Like bass drums pounding
Within me expanding outward
Is my craving for you
Delicate like a flute
Whispering within the ear
Yet strapping
Immutable
As cymbals obliterating silence
Angels hush their song
When your vocals fill the room

## Trapped in an Embrace

Bodies intertwined
Our scent fills the room
Its love
Saccharine
Deep within you
I find myself
You willingly allow yourself
To be intoxicated
Dehydrated
You request to drink me
We are trapped
In the embrace
Of
This thing we call love

## Morning

Morning sunshine
I hope your slumber was peaceful
And
Your dreams
Were of me
Gazing beyond your eyes
Deep within your soul

**Goddess**

The understanding of your love
Transforms my inhibitions
Into fathomless wealth
You make me more
Than I could be alone
Your nature is to fill my cup
Until it overflows
My desire is to lift you up
Fill you with joy
Allowing you to see yourself
As I see you
A goddess
Among us

**Your Fingers**

Your embrace
Like the heat of the sun on my face
The hair on my skin
Provide reverence to you
They stand at attention
When your fingers
Find their path up and down my spine
Awakening passion and desire for you

**Consume Me**

The perfume of wild cherries and lavender fills the air
As candles burn slowly across the room
The flickering flame reflects in the mirror
Gently illuminating your eyes
You smile at me invitingly
The touch of satin, silk and feathers
Against the skin
Awakens the imagination of many possibilities
You offer a taste of what is to come
I receive your gift of expression
No boundaries to unbound
Just your selfish desire to consume me...

## This Pill Called Love

If there was a pill that could change
The complex combination of chemical reactions within the brain
That we call love
Would you take it?
What is in us that produces
This complex combination of chemical reactions?
Is love more than this?
Can love be this simply explained?
Would you take a pill to remove this sensation?
Would you try to recreate what was lost however long ago?
Seeing someone at first glance who initiates
This complex combination of chemical reactions within the brain
Is it enlightening to the senses?
Does it bring joy
Anticipation
Fear
Or
Frustration?
Would you take this pill?
Why?

# heart·ache

pronounced: 'härt,āk

*noun*

1. emotional anguish or grief, typically caused by the loss or absence of someone loved.

## Fall from Favor

My fall from favor within your eyes
Was not entirely my doing
Eyes blinded by seduction
Greener grass without watering
Wanting more
Yet unwilling to create
Unable to see contributions of past and present glory
Desires heightened
Entertaining proposals of forbidden fruit
Once tasted
Adrenalin awakened
Excitement facilitated by the release of endorphins
Analgesia travels through the body
Numbing the pain receptors within the brain
Softening the blow of betrayal
Once the forbidden fruit is savored and consumed
The return of what was is no more
The Treachery
The Deception
The Lie
Has its reward
Both excellent and horrific
My fall from favor within your eyes
Was not entirely my doing
Your path chosen
You must now walk alone

**Now…I Must Let You Go**

Standing in the midst of loss
I wondered where to go next
Why would you not fight to keep our family together?
Fight to make it work somehow?
Fight to keep this family whole?
Why did I
When you replaced me with another?
I must now let you go to move on somehow
I gave all of me but it did not matter
Everything you asked of me
I gave
Whatever you needed from me
I provided
I must let you go
I cannot stay, see you, hear your voice and not be with you
I am strong but not that strong
My love for you was too great
You did not love me
Like I loved you
My love for you was as I loved myself
You have never and will never understand
The giving of my love is and has always been a rare thing
Time to move forward
The space has allowed me to move forward
I had to cut out my heart
Leave it behind
Emptied the blood vessels containing the spoiled and blemished blood
I had to grow a new heart in its place
Replacing the pillars of my foundation with liberty
Plowed the field with love of self
Fertilized with the truth of spiritual awareness
And planted the seeds within fertile soil in which
New love could flourish

**My eX**

Thank you for setting me free
You walked away when I could not
My soul was broken
I was lost
and alone
Until I found me
Thanks to you
The man I am now awake
The man I was
Lost so long ago
The discovery of my freedom in
The expression of my words
Thank you for setting me free
Allowing me to find me
Forcing me to find expressions of self
To find love
To express love
To find truth
To live truth
Anger and frustration were my closest companions
My eyes now opened
Liberty wonderful
Freedom so sweet
Honesty is my friend
To stand in the mirror naked
Examining my flaws, shame, sorrow and regret
I water my soul with dewdrops from above
Allowing God's grace to embrace me
That energy within us all was set free
In the fruit I now produce
from fertile soil
I was forced to labor
Alone
The love I now give is all encompassing

Free
Real
Honest and true
My roots well-grounded by the river of God's love
Drawing strength each and every moment
Providing shade from the harsh sun
My fruit nourishes many souls
Who knew such beauty would be found in such sorrow?
A diamond in the rough I sparkle
Thank you for freeing my soul
There is now liberty through the expressions of my ever-healing words

## Solitude

The spacious plot of solitude
Is the loneliness of missing you
Far from me
I long to hear your voice
See your smile
Enjoy your aroma
Taste your lips
Time sits still
Fueling my sorrow
My anguish
My torment
My suffering
I sit in glorious anticipation
Of my lover's return
The exquisiteness of awaking beside you
Is overshadowed by our separation
I take comfort
In the destruction of my solitude
Where once again I shall feel your embrace

# bless·ed

pronounced: blest,'blesid/

*adjective*

1. made holy; consecrated.

*noun*

1. those who live with God

**Give Love**

When you look
To your left
You see suffering and pain
When you look
To your right
You see those who pretend
When behind you
Is devastation
When all hope
Seems lost
In your darkest hour
Hold fast to who you are
In your faith
For
Challenges exist
To build character
Keep faith and hope
Give Love freely
Even when it hurts
Give love
And
You see the glory that is to come
You will see the limitless possibilities
Of God's creation
Within you

## Change

Finding yourself when surrounded by darkness
Is a challenge we all face from time to time
Looking within to find your foundation
Is the beginning of the process
If you do not start with your foundation
You will not be able to build something of value
Your value of self has nothing to do with external forces
It is a representation of the foundation within you
The challenge is the deconstruction of what was
To allow what needs to be
We sometimes fear
The unknown of the new
We know what was
Intimately
We want change but fear the unknown
At times there is comfort in what we know
Even if we don't like it
We may fall at times
But stand up
Dare to fight the fear
Force the change
Ask for help
Find the beauty in your change
Construct a new foundation based on liberty
And God's love

**Learn to Listen**

The overwhelming
Invisible force
That created the universe
And all within
It
Drives our life
It is the most powerful force
You could tap into
This force set the planets in motion
It caused the continuous expansion of the universe
It drives you and me
Pushing us to be better today than yesterday
It is the quiet still voice in the back of your mind
Highlighting right from wrong
It is what we know
We should do
Even when we do not do
It is the power that drives you
To achieve
As you get in the flow
When you listen to
The still quiet voice
You will see the unimaginable become tangible
Right before your eyes
Open yourself
And accept
The significances of this power
Only then will you
See His impact in your life
And be able to

Release your potential
And free your mind
For this power can do
Exceedingly abundant things
Above any thought or dream
You can envision
Learn to listen to the voice that is
God

**Let Go, Let God**

I believe in a world where people focus on doing the right thing
For their fellow citizens of planet earth
No matter how they treat you
No matter what their point of view
As you focus on doing good to those around you
God will open up the windows of paradise
And
Return that goodness to you
Let go of the past
Let go of the pain, the fear
The need to protect yourself from others
The sadness
Whatever binds you
Let it go
Yes
It is hard
So what?
The sidewalk is hard yet we all must walk on it
The Question is..
Where is your sidewalk taking you?
Suck it up
Be free, be open
We all want to be filled with His goodness
Yet we are not willing to empty our vessel first to allow ourselves to be re-filled
Let go of the pain and suffering that binds you
Let it go!
Where is it taking you?
If what you are doing is not working, do something different
Something new
Make the change

The past is gone
And can never be changed
Tomorrow is not yet written
Today is the only day you can control
Let go of the past
Let God take over
Just
Let go
And
Let God

**Beauty in the Fall.**

Standing in the midst of your adversity
You may not see the glory that is to come
Sometimes a fall is needed to remind you
Of the beauty that is God
How can one appreciate the horizon from the mountain top
If you never struggled to climb the mountain?
If you have never been to the valley?
How can you appreciate its warmth and abundance?
Life is in a state of perpetual movement
Continuously moving forward
Even when you don't see the light
Move forward
Pulling yourself out of the darkness may seem a tall order
Remember in order to know the light you must experience darkness
However,
You don't have to live in darkness
Pull yourself up out of the darkness
Find the beauty in the light of God

## Anticipation

In spite of what surrounds my life
At this juncture
I continue to look to the Heavens
With anticipation
Of what God
Has in store for my future
With great
Hope
Peace
Humility
Faith
And the fortitude
Necessary to succeed

## He Takes the Lead

The connection we continue to create with each other
Is facilitated through the sharing of God's truth
The truth that abides within our soul
Speak the truth
Keep it real
Keep it strong
and
Others will follow
As He leads

## Embrace Gifts

The understanding of self
Is the beginning of awareness
To the gifts God has loaned to you
Embrace your gifts
Become one with them then share them with the world
Allow the will of God
To be fulfilled within you
And the world will see goodness
We are all connected
We all desire goodness within our lives
We strive for good things
To do good
To share goodness
But at times we allow fear
And memories of a bygone time
To hold us back from sharing our goodness with others
I strive each day
To embrace the gifts
God has loaned to me
And
Share them with the world

**Blessings and Love**

There is a time in your life when a choice is required
And you need the fortitude to make it
When you look over the life you lived thus far
Are you where you thought you would be?
When you look to the future
What must you do to end up where you want to be?
Is there a magic formula that exists for happiness that escapes us all?
Is happiness a reality?
How do you create happiness out of adversity?
When you have fallen to the ground
When sadness prevails and the hardness that is life is exposed
When all hope seems lost
When the sun seems to never come out from behind the dark clouds
In these moments
Remember
There is hope
There is God
There is love
When we look to the left, He is there
When we look to the right, He is there
He has never left us alone
The good we do He returns to us in ways we may not understand
When we need Him
He is there
He provides us an outlet
He provides the answer
He gives us what we need when we need it
Our job is to stand in the fortitude of His love
Do good even when it hurts
Love with childlike faith
And
He will open the windows of Heaven
And
Give to you what you gave to others
Many times over

Our job is to receive the blessing without turning it away
The hardest part at times for us
Is to know how to recognize and receive
His blessings
And
Love
When it comes back to us
His ways may not be our ways but
His love is true
It is always there for us
Stand strong in the love He has given to you
Recognize and receive His blessings
Daily

**May God, May He, May You**

May God open both your eyes
That you may see
The beauty that exists within your life
May He remind you continuously
Of the love
That exists around you
May He brighten your path
Show you the way to create your heart's desires
May you be open as He enlightens you
And delivers knowledge of your purpose on this planet earth
And delivers His vision for you to your eyes

## Self-Fulfillment

When you look to others
To fill the needs in your life
You sell yourself short
If I do not live up to your expectations
And do not fill your need
Then you are the only one
Who is blameworthy
After all
It is your expectations you wished I could fulfill
Take the time to recognize
God gave you the answer
It is within your spirit
Your soul knows
You are enough to fill your needs
God made you complete all by yourself
I attempt to live my life
With the expectation of freeing others
From my expectations

**When the Hour is Dark**

When the hour is dark
When the sun is hidden behind the clouds
When standing before you
Is the mountain you must ascend
You may wonder
Where to turn within the darkness
Remember
What you need is already provided
Good friends you can call on in the middle of the night
Family who love unconditionally
Even strangers
To offer aid
Recognize the blessings that are already before you
Stand strong
Within the love that surrounds you
Ask for assistance
And
Be brave enough to receive

## Winds of Change

The winds of change are at work
Continuously blowing within our lives
Can you feel them?
Do you hear them?
God is blowing His cosmic wind all around us
If you listen you will hear
If you allow His wind to fill your sail
It will take you to new and exciting places
Embrace the challenges of life
Hurry to your fears with urgency
Draw it close
Removing all restriction holding you back
Allow the evolution
That is being accomplished within you
Take hold of your change
If not
Your fate is
To replicate the struggle
Until you acquire the lessons
God is teaching you

**Waters of My Soul**

The waters of my soul
Run deeply
They are many rivers
They shape the landscape as they flow
Immovable objects become sculpted into works of art
The nutrients dissolved within my waters
Brings life and fertility to wastelands
The many fruit trees surrounding my riverbank
Provide shade and sustenance
For weary travelers
They rest, consume, are refreshed and satisfied
The fish from my stream
Are enough to feed the nation
I overflow my banks
To fertilize farmer's fields
With passion
I am
Relentlessly driven forward
Each drop of water
Seeks to be one
With the ocean
That is God

**Magnificence Overwhelming**

The overwhelming
Magnificence
Wondrousness
That is the power of God
Is present in our lives
So busy
We are unable to see
The splendor God offers to us
Obscured by the noise that surrounds us
We lose the ability to sit in silence
To listen and hear what God is saying to us
We miss the gifts being offered
I seek to sit in silence daily
To listen
To hear
And continue to receive
The blessings being offered

## Stand Strong

God is always willing
It is our ability
To withstand the storm
That is being tested
Stand strong
Like a tree planted by the river
Holding on never letting go
Sometimes your job is to be steadfast
Just holding on
Knowing you are never alone
God is always with you
And He provides
All you need

## Replace? Fix.

We replace, replace, replace
Instead of spending time to fix what is broken
Fixing seems to be a thing of the past, from the days of old
Imagine if God
Was to turn His back on us
When we failed Him
Imagine if He decided to stop loving
As we do to each other
In our sorrow and pain
We cry out to Him for help
Yet we are unwilling to be like Him and fix what is broken
He loved us until death
Yet we run to protect ourselves from one another
How can we expect Him to forgive us
When we are not willing to be like Him
And love as He loves
Especially when it hurts
Love will cover a multitude of sins
If we let it

# in·spire

pronounced: in'spīr/

*verb*

1. to stimulate to action, to motivate
2. breathe in (air); inhale

## The Phoenix

Like the Phoenix
The flames of life renew me daily
The inferno that surrounds me
Destroys the impurities within my character
The fires do not dictate the man I am or become
The flames of life are the fuel
That replenishes my soul
The man I am
Is the man I choose to be
Standing in my desire to be better
In the midst of the inferno
I choose to be fearless

**Seize the Day**

Stay focused on your goals
Be true to you
To those around you
Face your fears
Slay the pink elephant in the room
Then get rid of the corpse
Allow others to be themselves
Treat them accordingly
The only one you have control of is you
Take control
Clutch the moment
If not today
Then when?

**Focus**

As the sun begins to light your path
Darkness and dismay
Shall lose its hold on your life
Stay focused
On the landmarks
As they become illuminated
Learn the lesson in the challenge
And you will keep the darkness behind you

**Dare to Dream**

The essence of who you are
Who you will become
Begins with a dream
When you lose your ability to dream
When you lose your vision
How do you know where you are going?
How do you stay on the path
Without a dream?
Dare to dream
Teach others to dream
The amazing possibilities of life
Are created within the dream
Dare to dream
And you will see amazing things
Created from nothing

## Take Inventory

As you take inventory of your life
You see the changes you fought
And eventually embraced
Hold fast as those seeds of change
Begin to deliver sweet fruit
You may not know where the winds of change
Are blowing you
But stay in the current
With your eyes to the sky
Listening to your inner
Man
Woman
Child
God
Embrace all that has started in you
Get ready to share
And eat
From the harvest of your labor
Are you ready?

## Prophecy

Your ability to face what life tosses your way
Is a representation of your belief
The development of who you are
Is a self-fulfilling prophecy
What you believe you can or cannot achieve
Your mind will create
Any and everything
You choose to believe
I choose to believe
I will reach the stars

**Release the Fear**

How much time will pass before you decide to say
What should have been said a long time ago?
If you don't say it
Then who?
Why wait?
What are you waiting for?
As you sit staring into the eyes of another
Holding back the feelings
Holding back the affection
Holding back the love
Don't you see everyone is doing the same thing?
Holding back...
If just one of us was to let go of the fear
And share ourselves selflessly
We would see the beauty of love, friendship, clarity
And the reality that as humans
Our needs are all connected
How much time will you let pass
While you miss out on something amazing
By not saying what should have been said so long ago?
Say I am sorry
Forgive me
And
Just let go

## The Lesson of Life

The evolution of life
Happens before our very eyes
The relentless current
Unfolds its diagram
There are no coincidences
Within the plan
The universe expands
As the laws of life dictate
Continuously moving forward
With purpose
Driven by growth and development
We enter
And
Depart
Each other's lives
For reasons
Not always conceivable at times
As we learn to embrace
The lessons of life
And
Face challenges
The beauty within our character
And the lessons are revealed

## Use Knowledge to Create

The ability to create something out of nothing
Is what separates
Success from failure
The ability to live out your true potential
Attaining what you want
Is related to your focus
Focusing on the prize
Is the only way to achieve the goal
Enjoy the journey and the potential that exists
Create it
Anew
Each day
Renew it
Each moment
Remember you have been given
The knowledge
To create something out of nothing
Use that knowledge
To create

## Understand to be Understood

Be slow to anger
Seek first to understand another
Rather than to be understood
This way you will harvest the fruit from another's soul
The soul knows the truth
It feels, seeks and understands truth
We often seek to be understood first
Whilst losing knowledge
And obtaining shame
When listening is not your path
Feed your soul understanding
Only then will
Wisdom will be your escort

## Exalted

Pressing toward the goal
When the goal is not in sight
This legacy
Those who have gone before us
Have laid down for us
I will not stand on their backs
To obtain my prize
But am grateful
To be exalted
Upon their shoulders
To reach the stars

## A New Thing

I woke up this morning with a spring in my step
With a sense of liberty from the world
I know not why
But there is an excitement building within me
Beyond words
A new thing has started within me
I no longer fight the flow
I allow the current that surrounds me
To carry me
To take hold of my life
Following the path that is being revealed
Day by day
No expectations
Only openness
And
The anticipation of this amazing new journey

# GIVE THE GIFT OF POETRY

If you enjoyed this book, feel free to buy another copy or two and give them away as gifts.

Visit

www.VictoriaViennaPublishing.com/PatrickMorris

And enter promo code: *givethegift*

For a 10% discount when you purchase two or more copies

To learn more about Patrick Oliver Morris, please visit the author website at

www.PatrickOMorris.com